THE BLACK IQ TEST

(Intelligence Quotion)

This test was composed, compiled, written, and produced by

Booty Adams - Researcher, Chronobiologist, Composer, Triple O.G.

©1999-2020 Booty Adams

DEDICATION

This textbook is dedicated to the staff of the Nubian Network and blackconsciousness.com, whose research, commitment, loyalty, and love for Black people made the **BLACK IQ TEST** possible. This test was composed with a little bit of soul, some hip-hop, some rock & roll, some country, some spiritual beats, and a whole lot of jazz.

It will not increase anyone's credit score or get anyone into any systemic, racist institutions, but it may return humanity and self-esteem to people who have lost their cultural bearing in recent times.

This test was composed to get this information to at least one billion+ people with a heavy emphasis on homeschooling, book clubs, classroom settings, workshops, and those seeking empowerment through study, research, and willpower. It is a must-read for athletes, musicians, entertainers, activists, students, homeboys, and homegirls, with no emphasis on classism, colorism, sexism, racism, or xenophobia. The desire is for Black people globally to one day rest in peace and power with our ancestors. RIPP!

HELPFUL PREP-TEST ILLUSTRATIONS

CONTENTS

INSTRUCTIONS

This test has 60 questions and is best taken
with pencil and paper. Taken with pencil and
paper gets the best results but is not
mandatory. This test is a tool and not about
instant gratification. At the end, you can
grade yourself. Black honor applies.
Please time yourself.
The test should take no more than 1 hour.
Answers are provided
at the end of the test. This test is to heighten
awareness and not to be considered a holy
book or the last answer. Take nothing for
granted and do your research and cross
checking.
This test should only be taken doing chill-time, where you can
grind and afterwards turn up!
This test is not meant to be a source of pressure.
Take it as many times as deemed necessary for those seeking to
help their people to globally believe in themselves once again!

WE ARE ALL WE GOT!

THE BLACK IQ TEST

MULTIPLE CHOICE QUESTIONS – CHOOSE ONE

1) WHICH COUNTRY HAS THE LARGEST BLACK POPULATION?

   a) BRAZIL
   b) the UNITED STATES
   c) INDIA
   d) NIGERIA

2) WHICH TEXT IS THE BASIS FOR ALL RELIGIOUS TEXTS OF TODAY?

   a) THE OLD TESTAMENT
   b) THE CABALA
   c) THE BOOK OF COMING FORTH
   d) THE KORAN

3) IN WHICH DIRECTION DOES THE NILE RIVER FLOW?

   a) EAST TO WEST
   b) NORTH TO SOUTH
   c) SOUTH TO NORTH
   d) WEST TO EAST

4) WHICH COUNTRY HAS THE LARGEST LAND PYRAMID ON EARTH?

   a) MEXICO
   b) the UNITED STATES
   c) EGYPT
   d) CHINA

5) WHICH COUNTRY HAS THE LARGEST AMOUNT OF INCARCERATED BLACK MEN AND BLACK WOMEN?

   a) SOUTH AFRICA
   b) THE UNITED STATES
   c) ENGLAND
   d) AUSTRALIA

6) THE 1ST DYNASTY OF WHAT IS NOW CHINA WAS BLACK, WHICH ONE?

    a) SHANG
    b) CHOU
    c) MING
    d) HAN

7) THE FIRST 10 PHARAOHS IN THE NILE VALLEY REIGNED FROM?

    a) EGYPT
    b) NUBIA
    c) SONGHAI
    d) GHANA

8) WHAT WAS THE QUEEN OF SHEBA'S NAME?

    a) SHEBA
    b) MAKEDA
    c) HATSHEPSUT
    d) NZINGA

9) THIS INDEPENDENT CLAN OF AFRIKANS ESCAPED SLAVERY TO FORM STRUCTURED COMMUNITIES IN THE CARIBBEAN, LATIN AMERICA, AND THE UNITED STATES?

    a) MESTIZOS
    b) MAROONS
    c) MAZOMBOS
    d) MULATTOS

10) WHICH AFRIKAN GODDESS WAS THE CITY OF PARIS NAMED AFTER?

    a) MA'AT
    b) SEKHMET
    c) ISIS
    d) HATHOR

11) WHICH AFRIKAN QUEEN WAS EUROPE NAMED AFTER?

  a) EUROPA
  b) CLEOPATRA
  c) NEFERTITI
  d) NEFETARI

12) WHICH WAS THE DOMINANT (PERVASIVE) MESSAGE LEFT BY THE ANCESTORS?

  a) "KNOW THYSELF"
  b) "REGISTER TO VOTE"
  c) "PRAYER IS THE ANSWER"
  d) "FIND A GOOD JOB"

13) WHICH GROUP OF AFRIKANS MANAGED TO CIVILIZED EUROPE?

  a) THE OLMEC (Xi)
  b) THE MANDINGOS
  c) THE MOORS (MUURS)
  d) THE CARTHAGENIANS

14) WHICH ORGAN PRODUCES THE HORMONE MELATONIN IN ABUNDANCE?

  a) BRAIN
  b) PINEAL GLAND
  c) HEART
  d) SKIN

15) ZULU ELDERS SAY THEIR ANCESTORS CAME TO AFRIKA FROM THIS PLANET?

  a) VENUS
  b) JUPITER
  c) SATURN
  d) MARS

16) AUSTRALIAN ABORIGINES WERE ONLY SUCCESSFULLY DEFEATED AND COLONIZED WHEN?

  a) MISSIONARIES WERE DEPLOYED WITH BIBLES AND CROSSES
  b) SOLDIERS LANDED WITH SUPERIOR WEAPON TECHNOLOGY
  c) DRUGS WERE DISTRIBUTED
  d) THEIR WATER SUPPLY WAS POISONED

17) WHICH RIVER WAS EARLIER CALLED THE RIVER OF ISIS?

  a) THE OHIO RIVER
  b) THE MISSISSIPPI RIVER
  c) THE SUSQUEHANNA RIVER
  d) THE BLACK WARRIOR RIVER

18) AUSTRALIAN ABORIGINALS CALL THIS ACTIVITY A RELATIONSHIP WITH THEIR ANCESTRAL PAST?

  a) A SIESTA
  b) DREAM TIME
  c) MARTI GRAS
  d) A FESTIVAL

19) WHAT WAS THE NORTH AMERICAN CONTINENT CALLED BY MANY OF ITS ORIGINAL INHABITANTS?

  a) TURTLE ISLAND
  b) AMERICA
  c) the UNITED STATES
  d) COLUMBIA

20) SANKOFA MEANS?

  a) WORKING FOR YOUR ENEMY FOR LIFE
  b) WE SHALL OVERCOME SOMEDAY
  c) PULLING YOURSELF UP BY YOUR BOOT STRAPS
  d) TO GO BACK AND FETCH ONE'S ESSENCE

21) THE 2 DEFINING CHARACTERISTICS OF THE AFRIKAN WAY?

a) HIGH CULTURE, DEEP THOUGHT
b) BUY LOW, SELL HIGH
c) IF YOU CAN'T BEAT THEM, JOIN THEM
d) APOLOGIZE AND COMPROMISE

22) PEOPLE OF COLOR OUTNUMBER COLOR-LESS PEOPLE ON THIS PLANET BY?

a) 10 TO 1
b) 2 TO 1
c) 5 TO 1
d) 3 TO 1

23) WHICH STAR SYSTEM DO THE DOGON ELDERS SAY ALL AFRIKANS COME FORTH FROM?

a) PLEIADES
b) SIRIUS (SIGI TOLO)
c) HYADES
d) ORION

24) THE BLACK DOT OR 3RD EYE IS STILL USED BY AFRIKANS TO ACQUIRE?

a) MONEY, POWER, AND RESPECT
b) STATUS IN FOREIGN LANDS
c) INNER VISION AND UNITY WITH LIGHT
d) MULTICULTURAL INTEGRATION

25) WHAT IS THE MAIN REASON BLACKS ARE BEATEN AND WHIPPED DURING COLONIZATION AND SLAVERY?

a) TO GET THEM TO WORK HARD
b) TO JUSTIFY THE ACTIONS OF THE OPPRESSOR
c) TO GET THEM TO LOSE THEIR AFRIKAN MINDS

  d) NO CIVIL RIGHTS LEGISLATION IS PASSED

26) THE AFRIKAN FAMILY INCLUDES?

  a) THE DEAD
  b) THE LIVING
  c) THE UNBORN
  d) ALL THE ABOVE

27) WHICH GROUP WAS THE EARLIEST TO ENSLAVE AFRIKANS?

  a) ENGLISH
  b) DUTCH
  c) PORTUGUESE
  d) ARABS

28) WHICH RIVER IN INDIA WAS NAMED AFTER AN ETHIOPIAN GENERAL?

  a) THE INDUS
  b) THE BRAHMAPUTRA
  c) THE NARMADA
  d) THE GANGES (GANGA)

29) THE "DIASPORA" IS BEST DESCRIBED AS?

  a) THE VARIOUS LANDS THAT AFRIKANS WERE SCATTERED TO OUTSIDE THE MOTHERLAND
  b) AN APPROACH TO CIVIL RIGHTS LEGISLATION FOR COLORED- MULTICULTURED PEOPLE
  c) THE URBAN GHETTO ECONOMY
  d) THE ILLUSION OF POWER IN BLACK POLITICS

30) IN 1700 BC, THE ARYANS CONQUERED THIS GROUP TO TAKE CONTROL OF THE INDUS VALLEY?

  a) SUMERIANS
  b) NEGRITOES

   c) DRAVIDIANS
   d) KUSHITES

TRUE OR FALSE QUESTIONS - CIRCLE ONE

31) THE ORIGINAL INHABITANTS OF THE UNITED STATES CALLED THEMSELVES INDIANS?

TRUE   FALSE

32) JOHN HANSON, A BLACK MAN, WAS THE FIRST PRESIDENT OF THE UNITED STATES?

TRUE   FALSE

33) THE 1ST AFRIKANS TO COME TO THE AMERICAS WERE SLAVES?

TRUE   FALSE

34) THE ORIGINAL BLACK INHABITANTS OF EGYPT CALLED THEIR EMPIRE KEMET?

TRUE   FALSE

35) ALL THE PHARAOHS OF THE NILE VALLEY WERE MEN?

TRUE   FALSE

36) MEN AND WOMEN OF COLOR HAVE BEEN OVERCOME AND VICTIMIZED BY COLOR-LESS MEN AND WOMEN?

TRUE   FALSE

37) EARLY AFRIKANS THOUGHT THE WORLD WAS FLAT?

TRUE   FALSE

38) SMALL BLACKS OCCUPIED EUROPE BEFORE CAUCASIANS?

TRUE   FALSE

39) MELANIN IS THE CHEMICAL SUBSTANCE THAT GIVES PIGMENT OR COLOR TO THE SKIN, THE EYES, AND THE HAIR?

TRUE   FALSE

40) BLACKS ARE STILL THE ONLY RACE THAT REFERS TO EACH OTHER COLLECTIVELY AS BROTHERS AND SISTERS?

TRUE   FALSE

41) BLACKS, LIKE EUROPEANS, ARE DESCENDED FROM THE ANIMAL KINGDOM?

TRUE   FALSE

42) BLACK WOMEN WERE CREATED FROM THE RIB OF A MAN?

TRUE   FALSE

43) THE RASTAFARI OF JAMAICA WERE THE 1ST BLACKS TO WEAR THEIR HAIR IN LOCS?

TRUE   FALSE

44) THE TERM "BLACK" ORIGINALLY REFERRED TO CORRECT THOUGHTS AND BEHAVIORS AMONG HUMAN BEINGS?

TRUE   FALSE

45) WITHOUT THE PRIVACY OF A LANGUAGE, AFRIKANS IN THE UNITED STATES DEVELOPED "EBONICS" AS A FORM OF COMMUNICATION?

TRUE   FALSE

46) "CHRIST CONSCIOUSNESS" MEANS RAISING ONE'S SELF TO A HIGHER LEVEL OF SPIRITUAL AWARENESS?

TRUE   FALSE

47) SICKLE-CELL IS NOT A DISEASE, BUT AN ENVIRONMENTAL ADAPTATION?

TRUE   FALSE

48) HEAVY MELANATED WOMEN SHOULD REFRAIN FROM EATING HIGH CONCENTRATIONS OF ANIMAL FLESH?

TRUE   FALSE

49) IGNORANCE OF THE HIGHER SCIENCES CAUSED WHITES TO NAME THE AFRIKAN EDUCATIONAL SYSTEM "THE MYSTERY SYSTEM"?

TRUE   FALSE

50) WHEN BLACKS ARE SOCIALIZED TO BE DEPENDENT; MONEY, EDUCATION, AND VOTING RIGHTS ARE GIVEN FREELY TO RULE AND CONTROL THEM?

TRUE   FALSE

51) EUROPEANS HAD COLLEGES AND UNIVERSITIES BEFORE THE PEOPLE OF AFRIKA?

TRUE   FALSE

52) ALKEBU-LAN WAS ANOTHER NAME FOR EUROPE?

TRUE   FALSE

53) NUBIA (TA-NEHISI) WAS THE ORIGIN OF EGYPTIAN HIGH-CULTURE?

TRUE   FALSE

54) BLACKS IN INDIA (UNTOUCHABLES OR DALITS) HAVE BEEN OPPRESSED BY A CASTE SYSTEM FOR OVER 2000 YEARS?

TRUE   FALSE

55) THE HAITIAN PEOPLE DEFEATED NAPOLEON'S ARMY IN BATTLE TO LIBERATE THEMSELVES?

TRUE   FALSE

56) THE SPIRITUAL REALM DOES NOT EXIST?

TRUE   FALSE

57) THERE ARE NOW MORE BLACKS THAT ARE ARAB THAN ANY OTHER TYPE DESIGNATED AS ARAB?

TRUE   FALSE

58) MENTAL SLAVERY KEEPS A PERSON AWAY FROM KNOWLEDGE AND MASTERY OF SELF?

TRUE   FALSE

59) IN THE SYSTEM OF GLOBAL WHITE SUPREMACY, NO PERSON OF COLOR CAN INTEGRATE ANY SITUATION WITHOUT WHITE PERMISSION?
TRUE   FALSE

60) THE ONLY WAY TO BEAT A SYSTEM IS WITH A SYSTEM?

TRUE   FALSE

STOP!

YOU HAVE REACHED THE END OF THE TEST!
PLACE PENS & PENCILS DOWN NOW PLEASE!

THE BLACK HONOR SYSTEM STILL APPLIES.
YOU ARE NOW READY TO GO OVER THE ANSWERS!

ANSWERS ARE LOCATED ON PAGE 21

THERE ARE APPROXIMATELY 60 QUESTIONS!
EACH QUESTION IS WORTH ONE POINT
CHECK THE PAPER YOURSELF

SCORE:_____

SCORES BELOW 30 SHOULD RETAKE THE TEST.

FAIR= 30

GOOD= 40

HIGH BLACK CONSCIOUSNESS IQ= 50+ CORRECT

THIS TEST IS BEING TAKEN WORLDWIDE.

DON'T TAKE ANY ANSWER FOR GRANTED. PLEASE DO RESEARCH FOR ALL THE

QUESTIONS. This test is not a HOLY BOOK or the LAST WORD!

VISIT A BLACK BOOKSTORE, CONSULT WITH YOUR FAMILY, FRIENDS AND

TEACHERS. TAKE IT TO THE INTERNET, SOCIAL MEDIA.

(The word QUOTION is used instead of the word QUOTIENT, due to the esoteric nature of this test. The global results cannot be counted, measured, or contained!)

THANK YOU ALL! You are appreciated.

STILL...CRITICISMS CAN BE E-MAILED TO:

nnetwork@blackconsciousness.com

DONATION CAN BE MAILED TO:

The NUBIAN NETWORK P.O. BOX 3578 Baltimore, Md. 21214

THE NUBIAN NETWORK'S WORLDWIDE

BLACK IQ SELF TEST
ANSWER PAGE

"THANKS FOR TAKING THE TEST"... BOOTY ADAMS

MULTIPLE CHOICE   TRUE OR FALSE

1) C	16) D	31) FALSE	46) TRUE
2) C	17) B	32) TRUE	47) TRUE
3) C	18) B	33) FALSE	48) TRUE
4) D	19) A	34) TRUE	49) TRUE
5) B	20) D	35) FALSE	50) TRUE
6) A	21) A	36) TRUE	51) FALSE
7) B	22) A	37) FALSE	52) FALSE
8) B	23) B	38) TRUE	53) TRUE
9) B	24) C	39) TRUE	54) TRUE
10) C	25) C	40) TRUE	55) TRUE
11) A	26) D	41) FALSE	56) FALSE
12) A	27) D	42) FALSE	57) TRUE
13) C	28) D	43) FALSE	58) TRUE
14) B	29) A	44) TRUE	59) TRUE
15) D	30) C	45) TRUE	60) TRUE

© 1999, 2020 Booty Adams

WARNING- unlike systemic racism, this information is not worth arguing, fighting, or killing anyone.

This test is not a competition. It is all about critical analysis.

Thanks for taking the test, research, and more research!

Send comments to: nnetwork@blackconsciousness.com

NOTES:

COMPOSER / AUTHOR QUOTES

TESTED

Booty Adams

"Every day you are tested. When you wake and rise you are tested. You are challenged. Life is not a trip, but it is a journey. The day you are not tested, is the day that you are dead. Count your blessings!"

RESEARCH

Booty Adams

"It's called research. It won't improve your credit score or get you a job, but at least you'll know a lot more about what you are worth as a human being."

Be sure to check-out

THE BLACK IQ TEST- 2ND TESTAMENT